DON'T WORRY
STOP SWEATING...
use deodorant!

DON'T WORRY
STOP SWEATING...
use deodorant!

RICHARD FEELGOOD, PH.D.
WITH RICHARD SANDOMIR, D.W.I.,
AND RICK WOLFF, E.I.E.I.O.

ILLUSTRATED BY HESHY QHROME

BARNES
&NOBLE
BOOKS
NEW YORK

Acknowledgments

The authors would have written this book without the following people, but we thought it would be nice to thank them anyway.

Our wives, Trish Wolff and Griffin Miller, who adroitly pick up our small stuff after us; our parents, who knew us as small stuff; Jean Zevnik, our editor, who recognized that this idea wouldn't stink; our agent, Joel Fishman, who convinced our editor that this idea wouldn't stink; Heshy Qhrome, our innovative illustrator, who can make small stuff sweat; John Rapoport, Esq., Mr. Big Stuff himself; Amy Einhorn, who came up with the deodorized title for this book; and Dale Carnegie, Norman Vincent Peale, Napoleon Hill, Deepak Chopra, and Wayne Dyer, without whom Dr. Richard Feelgood's derivative books would not exist.

Contents

Letter from the Publisher:
How to Use This Book

D r. Richard Feelgood wants to do more than help you. He wants to make his advice a sweat-free exercise in self-help. If you have to sweat his advice, then you're in deep trouble. Because believe me, it's simple.

And to guide you through the thicket of Dr. Feelgood's poppycock is Drippy the Elf, renowned less for his stature of small stuff than for his Brobdingnagian sweat glands.

You may never sweat again.

1.
Don't Sweat the Small Stuff . . .
Use Deodorant!

We all sweat about the little things in life. We get worked up. We yell. We get hives. We buy an Uzi. While you're carrying grocery bags to your car, someone steals your cart with the remaining bags, including the one filled with Velveeta. You rush after the thief, reciting Lucky's interminable soliloquy from *Waiting for Godot*, then wait until the Velveeta is safe in your arms.

You feel justified in your anger. But you're sweating. Whoa, Nellie, you smell so bad that octogenarian cloistered nuns flee from you in horror. Even if we don't want to admit that we sweat the small stuff, we need not smell like a Staten Island landfill in August.

Remember, there are whole departments

1

in drugstores for deodorants. They're prominently displayed and colorfully packaged, with eye-catching names like Secret and Speed-Stick. And keep in mind: don't buy the cheap ones that flake off under your pits. Without the good stuff, we're nothing but immigrants in steerage.

2.

Don't Worry, Eat Money

You like going out to lunch every day, you like getting out of the office, you like being served.

But wait—you're spending a lot of money. You spend $7.50 a day for lunch and a tip, so now you ask your wife to make one that costs about $2 a day. You've saved $5.50!

Multiply that by five times for thirty years, and you've got $100,000!

Sure, it's a bit tacky for a chief executive officer to share liverwurst sandwiches with pigeons. But you think it's a great image, which inspires you to kill health insurance, pension plans, and mileage payments for traveling salespersons.

Multiply that by 550 employees by 365 days a year by thirty years, invest in something that yields 8 percent annually, and you are richer than you can ever imagine!

Besides, those pigeons rarely complain, never call in sick, and never ask for a raise.

3.

Live This Day as if It Were Your Last—
It Might Be!

I remember one time I was counseling an inmate on Death Row. After years and years of throwing red tape into the system, his number was finally up. And there was no call coming in from the governor.

Not knowing what to say to him, I simply suggested, "You know, you ought to live this day as if it were your last . . ."

He looked up at me with his cold, murderous eyes, and said, "It is, you jerk! And the last thing I want to do is waste any of it looking at you."

With that, I quickly turned and sprinted out of the Big House. After all, who wants to hang out and listen to some depressing, gloomy guy who's ready to be croaked?

4.

Dr. Feelgood's Guide to
Feeling Good No. 1

1. Eat good food, and lots of it.

2. Touch yourself where it feels good. A lot.

3. Have money. A lot of it.

4. Don't work hard.

5. Become a therapist, discover
   stress is bad.

5.

Bon Appétit

Joe Schmidt, famed former head coach of the Detroit Lions, once assembled his troops before a game, and announced:

"Men, life is nothing more than a doody sandwich—and every day, you take another bite."

Trust me. Truer words were never spoken.

6.

Five Quick Ways to Relieve Stress in Your Everyday Life

1. Yell at the next stranger you meet on the street. Yell right in his face.

2. Don't go to work. Then tomorrow, when you go to the office, tell the boss you simply lost track of the days.

3. Be different. Men, grow a beard on only one side of your face. Women, shave only one of your legs.

4. Test your friends. Call them collect and feign ignorance when they ask, "Haven't you heard of 10-321?"

5. Get lots of money. Put it on the floor. Roll around in it.

7.

The Dummies' Guide to Sweating Small Stuff

No sweat at all .... Meeting someone for the first time and then promptly forgetting his or her name

Nervous trickle of sweat .... Forgetting your spouse's name

Mild perspiration .... Forgetting your next door neighbor's name, even though you've lived next door to him for fifteen years

Drenching sweat .... Forgetting your own name

8.

Keeping Your Small Stuff Clean

Most people agree that when their small stuff starts to accumulate grime, that's when you should start sweating. So here are some small stuff cleaning tips, straight from Heloise Jr.:

Gerbils .... Vaseline coats their fur quite nicely and the little varmints like its smooth ride.

Jockeys .... Cruex not only cleans them, but keeps them shiny in their saddles.

Electrons .... Brillo soap pads provide a rugged, random atomic workout and

they magnetize the wacky
particles, too.

Emmanuel Lewis .... Ivory soap. He likes to float downriver
on it.

9.

If Someone Throws You the Ball,
You Don't Have to Catch It

If I've learned anything, it's that we were not born to wipe up everybody's mess. That lesson became very personal to me one day when my grandma frantically called, interrupting my daily session with my financial adviser.

"Sonny, if I don't give them all my money, they won't let me stay in the home another day," she said, weeping. "Please help me."

"Hey, crazy lady, I ain't paying," I said, with love, of course. "What's wrong, you forget Merrill Lynch's 800 number, or something?"

My rant shook Granny from her stupor. She remembered her seven-figure investments in Microsoft and Intel, paid off her debts, died six months later, and left me her fortune.

So remember, a lot of fly balls will be hit your way in life. Most will conk you on the noggin. Face it, only a few of us can be Ken Griffey Jr. The rest of us just play like Steve Urkel.

10.

Adopt a Lot of Children through the Mail—on the Cheap

The most rewarding thing in my family's life is adopting children through the mail. We have 112 of them, at only $32 a month. We enjoy this because we never have to invite them home, never have to cook for them. Their grateful letters and sad-eyed photos are more than enough for us.

My seven-year-old son sends his adopted siblings Polaroids of his privileged suburban life and they send back stick-figure sketches of themselves. They're oh so brave in the face of poverty. The lessons of their correspondence will last my boy a lifetime—or at least until Sally Struthers's next doughnut feast ends.

The best feature of this setup is if you don't like an adopted kid after a year—say, her demands for towels or flip-flops grow unreasonable—you can trade up for a cuter or younger daughter.

When you adopt a child by mail, you get all the fun of helping a poor kid very, very, very far away—without a scintilla of responsibility.

All for the yearly price of *The New Yorker*! Yes, *The New Yorker*.

11.

Think of Your Armpits as
Major Sources of Life's Stress

It's tough trying to create a life of serenity when you smell like diapers that have been unchanged for three days. You may like the scent as your own personal aroma, but it's as welcome as hanging with Marlon Brando after an hour of binge eating. Hoowee! Memorable bouquet, eh?

If you don't use deodorant, you will be doomed to a life of minimum wage. If you don't use deodorant and wear polyester, you will be be no more welcome in a bank or school than a topless leper in the *Sports Illustrated* swimsuit issue.

And "You stink!" will be more than a comment on your lousy work.

(This advice is exempt for readers in Europe, where people sweat and smell naturally and even the pope occasionally reeks.)

I have devised my own personal views about today's popular deodorants and antiperspirants.

Right Guard	Worn by President Clinton throughout the Monica Lewinsky scandal. Seems to have worked well. Wonder what Hillary uses under her pits?
Five Day Deodorant Pads	Highly effective but mighty noticeable on the beach. But if you can stand the embarrassment, you'll feel like little fingers are being stuck in the dike of your pores.
Mitchum	A deodorant created by an actor who surely smelled after twenty hours on *The Winds of War*? Come on. And all that time he spent without air conditioning in the original *Cape Fear*?
Ban	Great name, but it was Dick Nixon's personal favorite. Interestingly, it worked under his arms, but despite his best efforts, it failed to work above his upper lip.

12.
Be Comfortable Knowing Nothing

There was once a land where the citizenry went mad when the sage could not answer their questions. One day the rich men told the wise man, "The stock market has crashed. Isn't this the worst thing that could have happened?"

The wise man replied, "I dunno. I'm no Alan Greenspan."

The next day, a nuclear bomb leveled the land. "We have no homes, no offices, no buy orders," the survivors said. "Isn't this the worst thing that could have happened?"

The wise man said, "I dunno. I just taught myself not to sweat the small stuff."

The survivors proclaimed, "The wise man is lower than toejam!"

When the worried masses learned that they knew no less than the wise man, they relied on themselves, not a nut job spouting nonsense aphorisms. They built a better society, minus

John Tesh. And late one night, they invaded the wise man's ashram and clipped his toenails against his will.

13.

Be Happy Where You Are ...
Because Nobody Else Will Be

Sadly, too many of us postpone our happiness, until we're too old or, for that matter, not breathing. We rarely realize that our moment is now, so we must seize the day, take time to smell the roses, play within ourselves, walk the walk, talk the talk. We can't simply say, "Someday will come."

That day is here. It's come. And it will be gone after *Nightline*.

We tell ourselves that we'll be happy when we get out of the iron lung, when we can trade welfare for workfare, when Dad stops drinking, when our stupid brother-in-law moves out, when our satellite dish is up and working again.

Meanwhile, life moves forward without your happy, vapid face. So buck up. Life could suck worse. You could work for George Steinbrenner. Mike Tyson could bite off your ear.

Understand this. There is no single path to becoming a happy moron. Just being a happy moron *is* the right path.

14.

Understand the Power of Money

A wise old philosopher once told me, "Look, no matter who you are, you're always going to have problems in life. But the truth is, problems are a lot easier to handle if you have lots of dough."

Think about that for a second, and you'll see that it's really true. There really is a direct correlation between how much you have in your bank account and how much easier it is to hurdle the obstacles in life. To illustrate this point, I've even designed a small chart that shows my personal growth as a function of my burgeoning income:

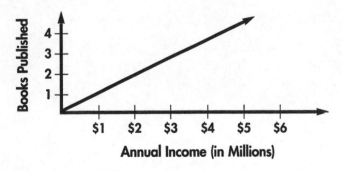

15.
Don't Worry, Make Money

My next book in this series is just what this essay preaches: "Don't worry, make money." The title is self-explanatory and easy to follow.

The well-known comedian Steve Martin used to do a routine in which he would tell people how to live like a millionaire.

"First," he would say, "you have to have a million dollars."

People would laugh at that simple wisdom. But believe me, it's true! Just look at this chart that my accountant put together for me:

Top Six Shrinks Who Don't Worry and Make Money

Rich Shrinks	1997 Earnings
Dr. Frasier Crane	$18 million
Dr. Richard Feelgood	14 million

Dr. Laura Schlessinger	$12 million
Dr. Deepak Chopra	9 million
Dr. Joyce Brothers	7 million
Dr. Bob Hartley	4 million

My only problem? Making more money than that self-absorbed twit, Crane. I'd better think fast—his syndication money will be rolling in soon.

16.

How the Idea that "More Is Better" Changed My Life

Afew years ago, I used to live across the street from a man who was intensely proud of how he was doing in business. We both lived in relatively modest homes, but whenever he got a big raise in salary or a big bonus, he couldn't wait to go out and buy a fancier car, add a new room to his house, build a swimming pool, or join the local country club.

I know all this because I watched him from my modest home across the street.

One day, I encountered my neighbor stepping out of his limousine, being dropped off at his front door. "Say, friend," I asked him, "I'm doing some research for a book I'm writing about the psychology of life."

My neighbor stopped, turned, and looked at me quizzically.

I then asked him, "Let me ask you this: Are you happy? I

mean, are you really, really happy?"

The neighbor laughed out loud, turned on his heel, and yelled back, "Sure I am! And remember—having more is definitely better!"

It was precisely at that moment I decided that if my first book became a national bestseller, I would immediately follow it with another bestselling book very much like the first one.

After all, I wanted a swimming pool, too. And a new addition to my house, too.

Yes, more is better.

17.

Just for Fun, Agree with Criticism of You

Once upon a time, I used to be arrogant, obnoxious, and haughty—a real know-it-all. As a psychologist, people would come to me in search of answers for their psychic pain and, quite frankly, I would get in their face and give it to them straight, whether they liked it or not.

For some reason, my patients did not like this approach. They would say, "You know, Richard, you're a real jerk." Or, "Richard, you're a moron." For many years, I simply decided to disregard these cockeyed criticisms. After all, they came from sniveling psychos.

I'M GOING TO LET
HIM THINK I'M A JERK.

But one day, I had a revelation. Instead of trying to dispense my psychological gobbledygook to one nutcase at a time, I realized that if I could write down my simplistic, "touchy-feely" directives in a small book, I could make a lot of money, reach a much larger audience, and have a lot more free time on my yacht.

So I did just that.

Now, while I'm not certain what the point of this story is, I do know that while I'm still arrogant, haughty, and obnoxious, I'm considerably wealthier: I have a three-book contract, a Dr. Feelgood line of Vermont psychotic teddy bears, and an advertiser-supported web site.

18.

Above All, Remember This . . .

Wayne Gretzky, the greatest hockey player of all time, once observed, "You know, in life and in hockey, you miss 100 percent of the shots you don't take. . . ."

Well, duh, Wayne. I guess that's why you're a hockey player.

19.

Do One Thing at a Time and You've Wasted a Lot of Time

The other day on the freeway, I saw a man who, in the blink of an eye, spoke on his cell phone, masturbated, read from *Finnegan's Wake*, chatted online with Ted Kaczynski, sang the unknown stanza from "The Star Spangled Banner," juggled a few cats, and changed his deodorant pads. All at seventy miles per hour.

What an exquisite frenzy of efficiency! What focus! Inspired, I started doing all sorts of things simultaneously, and I made an awful mess on the fabric of my leather car seat. But the point is, how much happier can a man be than when he does everything he loves, all at once?

I've seen people try to do one thing at a time. Walk, but not chew gum. Read the Torah, but not change the kitty litter. Watch a movie, but not talk loudly to the person beside him. Have sex, but not watch *Bewitched* on Nick at Nite.

My advice? Forget the stress generated by getting too little accomplished in a mere twenty-four-hour day. The old philosophy is still the best one: It's better to get things done badly than not at all.

20.

Make Peace with Imperfection

Without having to leave the comfort of your couch and your family-size bag of Doritos, it's not hard to find those absolute perfectionists out there whose lives are a constant search for inner peace.

There's always some meddling dumb-ass who just can't help him- or herself from interfering in your life. There's always somebody out there who just can't help digging in and cleaning up the mess on your desk at work, straightening up your closet at home, or taking it upon herself to throw out your lucky T-shirt. You know, the same T-shirt you've had since you were a junior in high school.

The other day, I went to my brother-in-law's for a cookout. He had just finished polyurethaning the rec-room floor, and he was showing it off. While he was outside cooking on the grill, my kid accidentally dropped a hammer and left a big dent on the shiny new rec-room floor.

My kid asked me whether we should say anything to

anybody. I looked around, saw that nobody was there, and simply shrugged it off.

"Hey," I told my son, "if nobody saw nothing, then nothing happened, right?"

We pulled a throw rug over where the dent was. Practice makes perfect.

21.

Dr. Feelgood's Guide to
Feeling Good No. 2

1. Paint a goatee on the corpse of someone you hated.

2. Don't bother to open mail from Ed McMahon—you didn't win.

3. Wear edible underwear to the health spa.

4. Play the oboe naked.

5. Tell your patients not to worry.

22.

Don't Move during a Circumcision (or You'll Miss the Good Cold Cuts)

This Buddhist adage, taught by the master Dalai Youngman, provides me with all the wisdom I could ever need.

The essence of this lesson is learning not to jerk like a neurotic putz during life's most difficult moments.

If you flinch during your circumcision, your member will be minus more than a little foreskin.

This ability to show complete composure in vexing situations will always help you. I remember being confronted by a Kodiak bear during a naked-hairy-man outing at a convention of blowhard pop psychologists. I stood stock-still for what seemed like an eternity until the bear pointed at my frightened, overcircumcised member, laughed, and left for meatier prey.

This tao of equanimity does not mean you should be passive

in the face of difficulties. Rather, it's a prescription for under-standing that unless you act correctly at tense moments, your cojones may say, Hasta la vista, baby!

23.

If . . .

I remember quite vividly what my grandpa once told me about his attitude in life when things weren't going his way, and his pithy thoughts have stuck with me all these years.

"Richie," Gramps would say to me, "If 'ifs and buts' were candy and nuts . . . then we'd all have a very merry Christmas."

And you know, to this day, I still have no idea what the hell that old goofball was talking about.

24.

See the Glass as Already Broken
(or Break It if You Have to, Damn It)

There is an old Latin saying that allows me to accept bad things as they happen. It translates roughly to this: "Excrement happens, so duck." (It's dirtier in Latin, but I've cleaned it up.) The essence of this pithy nugget helped me form an awareness—even numbness—to the horrible vagaries of everyday life, so that when the worst that could happen happened, I was prepared.

I knew my first girlfriend would dump me like I had Legionnaires' disease. I knew my partner would steal all our pension money. I knew Helen Gurley Brown wore a wig, I knew William Shatner wore a wig, but Marv Albert? I was shocked! Shocked!

I know everything and everyone I have ever loved, eaten, worn, or valued will spoil, crumble, fade, or be taken from my car.

Peace can be achieved only when you expect nothing to

last. Sure it's depressing, but it's practical. If you're frozen in horror by the sight of Visigoths tossing your precious Baccarat glass slippers against the wall, then you don't understand the philosophy. Once you can put the philosophy into practice, you'll be grateful for the time you spent with your precious Baccarat, for the time Abe Lincoln sipped Hawaiian Punch from it, and for the time Courtney Love sipped blood from it.

25.

Dwarves Don't Like to
Be Called Small Stuff

When I addressed the annual conference of Dwarves Who Write Mumbo-Jumbo Pop-Psych Books on how not to sweat the small stuff, I mistakenly called them "small stuff."

"We're little people!" they shouted.

"And don't call us midgets, either," they added.

"Or munchkins! We don't even get residuals!"

As I looked down at them—their little feet not even long enough to dangle from their chairs—I became even more resolute in my belief. Of course they're small stuff!

Tiny, itsy-bitsy stuff. Teensy-weensy hands and toes.

"Hey, small stuff," I responded. "Can you hold hands with a seven-footer without being carried aloft?"

Of course, all they could do was grumble in their teeny-tiny voices. Naturally, I wasn't going to sweat this small stuff.

They couldn't deny me the right to call stuff "small stuff," which is obviously the correct sobriquet.

Did I sweat their protestations? Never, shorty.

26.

Drive as if You Lived in
Boca Del Ray Vista, Florida

In a retirement community, nobody drives over twenty-five miles per hour and accidents are never fatal.

A pileup of ten cars rushing to Manny's Low-Fat Diner and Outpatient Clinic in Boca Del Ray Vista on May 18, 1996, caused no injuries except for leaks in the drivers' Depends.

Recently, I drove from Philadelphia to New York as if I were a seventy-eight-year-old retiree, traveling I-95 at twenty-five miles per hour in the right lane. Many drivers darted inconsiderately in front of me, gestured rudely, and tried to run my 1967 Rambler off the road.

Yet driving at thirty-five miles per hour or slower delivered inner peace as I'd never known it. Others vented rage around me, but I drove blissfully as if Bo and Peep were my copilots to Heaven's Gate. Driving has become less a means to get somewhere, and more a way to breathe deeply, to force others to go slowly and think deeply, and to reflect on how rich and powerful I am.

27.

Five Quick Steps to Instant Wealth

1. Play Lotto. Pray that you win.

2. Look out the window to see if Ed McMahon is coming to your door.

3. Write a bestselling self-help book (or two).

4. Marry somebody who just won Lotto.

5. Marry Ed McMahon. He does it frequently.

28.

Practice Ignoring Other People's Thoughts

It has been estimated that the average human being experiences 50,000 thoughts per day. If you have meaningful encounters with eight people a day, that's 450,000 thoughts. And 95 percent of them are bound to be infantile or homicidal or as focused on hazardously large-breasted women who love hip-hop on *The Jenny Jones Show*.

To experience the perfect sweatless day, you must learn to dismiss the many insipid thoughts that come your way, and learn to caress your *very* important ideas.

When bad thoughts invade your brain space, remember: they are harmless unless conceived by intelligent people, who are rarer than ever today. So if a doltish thought—such as, "You're a lousy CPA, you lost one million dollars for me, and your panty hose has runs in it"—

occurs to you, ignore it and it will vanish. I guarantee it.

If I let vapid thoughts interfere with my brain processes, I couldn't have written this vapid, totally derivative book!

29.

Relax, You Miserable Slug

What does it really mean to relax? To some, it means shutting off the alarm clock and oversleeping for work. For others, relaxation means swinging in a hammock.

They would all be right. Anything that removes you from the frenzy of everyday life is a plus. At life's most stressful moments, you should always back off and loiter.

You've got an important 9:15 A.M. presentation on a new account? Take a nap. Slept past ten o'clock? Don't worry! Everybody respects the wide-eyed, relaxed superachiever!

Feel stressed performing that vasectomy? Sweating like the dearly departed Chris Farley? Hands shaking? Kick back. Take a walk, light up a smoke, have a beer. Trust me, that flaccid fellow whose scrotum you're about to cut into will thank you later.

He might even give you a tip.

30.

Remember, There Is a Way to
Dust for God's Fingerprints

Rabbi Andrew Sipowicz reminds us that much of what God has created can be booked, printed, and photographed in three distinct poses. If everything in the world has God in it, then it can be dusted for His fingerprints.

Sure, it's easy to say God's hand is in flowers, meadows, kittens, waves gently lapping a sandy shore, the smile of a beautiful child, or Godiva chocolates.

But it's less easy to admit that God is in the assault, the murder, or the Brinks' armored car heist.

Yet, He and His prints are there. And when correctly dusted, His thumb print looks like this:

31.

Wait for Perspiration, Not Inspiration

Some sage once said a great deed is the result of 10 percent inspiration and 90 percent perspiration. Or maybe it was 20 percent and 80 percent. Or 30–70.

Well, that's wrong. I've discovered that it's easy enough to get inspired. It happens to me all the time. How much inspiration do you think was required to think of fifty-nine good ideas for this book?

No, the hard part was summoning up the perspiration. I'm not a sweater. I don't work out. I avoid hot climates. My house is air-conditioned, including the garage, the attic, and the bathrooms. So except when I rush from my car to my office, I rarely encounter heat.

To access my inner sweat, I simply must wait. We must be willing to admit that "no sweat will drip before its time," and that the eventual oozing of perspiration that will stain my T-shirt will be worth the wait. By simply learning that perspiration has its own rhythms, you will guarantee that it will come—and in most cases it will gush forward into view when you're raising your arm in class to answer a question.

32.

Ask for What You Want (and What the Hell, Ask for What Your Friends Want, Too)

I'm always happy to help people, especially people I don't know, and especially if they ask me where they can buy my books. In fact, it is my experience that most people not only want to help you if you ask, but they'll thank you for asking.

We fear people will say no, but we insult them if we arrogantly and incorrectly assume they don't want to help.

Bill D., a patient, learned my advice worked. One day, he told his boss, "Stan is doing a lousy job. His body odor is making it tough for us to work. Would you fire him, please?"

Bill's boss thought ill of Stan, but hadn't thought of firing him. But Bill was polite, sincere, had a good work record, and brought incriminating photographs of Stan. Within minutes, Stan was out on his bony ass.

33.

Interrupt Others . . . or They'll
Finish Their Own Insipid Thoughts

It occurred to me a few years ago that I frequently interrupted others or finished their sentences, or both. What tremendous energy it takes to think for two people at once!

Maybe some Birkenstock-wearing woolly-headed shrink will tell you how rude and disrespectful it is to interrupt others who are drowning amid their verbal diarrhea. But I don't care. It's all I can do to shorten these woeful conversations and end my suffering.

One day, my good-for-nothing son-in-law wanted to join the local neo-Nazi, skinhead branch of the Ku Klux Klan.

"It's a career move, Dad," he explained.

I listened to his spiel for two minutes—he recited from chapter four of *Mein Kampf*—and then I finished his last sentence for him by cracking him over the head with a Luger. End of conversation. It felt good. I felt good, too.

34.

Friends Come and Go. So What?

I often wonder why so many people become so emotional and teary-eyed at graduation ceremonies, going-away parties, retirement sendoffs, or when a family simply packs up and moves to another community.

"We'll never see our dear friends anymore!" they blurt out, as they wipe their runny noses on their sleeves. "We're best friends for life!!"

Rubbish. In my mind, as you go through life, you'll find that your friends are similar in many ways to disposable cigarette lighters. That is, they're both replenishable and replaceable. And no matter where you go in this country, you can always get more—friends or cigarette lighters.

That's just the way it is. So chill out, pack up, and move on.

35.

Five Quick Steps to Happiness

1. Buy my books.

2. Remember that it's always better to give than to receive.

3. Hence, buy several copies of my books. Give some to your friends and relatives.

4. Think pleasant thoughts. Think about buying more of my books.

5. Have a nice day.

36.
Dr. Feelgood's Guide to
Feeling Good No. 3

1. Call someone, preferably someone you don't know, and say, "I love you."

2. Spray other people's bowling shoes with Cheez-Whiz.

3. Don't wear underwear on a first date.

4. Hand out travel-size bottles of deodorant to subway riders on hot summer days.

5. Take your family's inner children to Disney World.

37.

Learn Democracy through the Small Intestine: Become a Proctologist

Bowels are life's great equalizers.

Proctology is a scientific form of highway supervision: Any detailed analysis of our butts will show that some work better, faster, or more efficiently than others. Yet we are more similar than different.

As proctologists peer into our tushes, they are really examining democracy at work, where everyone is truly the same where they sit, and where we can focus on what binds us, not what tears us apart.

Oh sure, some of us may have paved superhighways, some may have bumpy back roads. But any licensed practitioner will tell you we're all the same where it counts.

38.

Personal Happiness

You often hear people say that "money can't buy you happiness." From my experience, you might want to rethink that bit of so-called traditional wisdom a bit.

Trust me. I used to not have money. And . . . I wasn't very happy. I used to say to myself, "Gee, I'm not very happy. I wish I had more money."

But now, I do have money. And you know what? Today, I am very happy.

So these days, whenever I hear someone say, "Money can't buy you happiness," I simply assume that he doesn't have much money in his bank account.

Or at least not as much as I have. Remember—I have lots of money. And because of all that dough, I no longer have to sweat the small stuff. I can now pay someone to do it.

39.

To Make Your Point, Let Out Some Gas

This simple technique has worked wonders for everyone who's tried it. It has the impact of relaxing your body, increasing your focus, improving your digestion, and of course, it gets everybody's attention. In a hurry.

After all, how many times have you been to a cocktail party where everyone was too busy talking, all chatting at the same time, all trying to get in their latest piece of gossip? It seems that in our busy, overworked society today, everybody has simply forgotten how to kick back, take a load off, and relax.

It appears that we are still hell-bent on getting our fifteen minutes of fame. We still desperately want everybody else to stop in midsentence, turn around, look at us, and recognize us for those distinctive, unique talents that place us above the common riffraff.

Let me assure you from personal experience that there's simply no better way to get heads to turn in a crowded room than by expressing yourself from the very bowels of your soul.

At the very least, you'll clear some room to the bar. Plus, you'll give everybody else something to talk about.

40.

Be Aware of What You Don't Know, Because You Can Hire People to Do What You're Stupid At

As my wife read a report by the local medical ethics commission that recommended revoking my license to practice psychology, she told me, "Dr. Dickie, it's not important that you offer trite, unhealthy advice to your patients. It's important that you know you're a shmuck and you take the right action."

That advice sure opened doors for me! I came to grips with the reality that I was a lousy scholar, a lousy therapist, and a lousy writer. So I subcontracted my work out!

I hired Deepak Chopra to study for me, John Bradshaw to coach my therapy sessions, and Jack Canfield to ghostwrite my books, as if he were ladling out chicken soup for my bank account, real estate, and CDs.

Chances are you're good at certain things and not very good

at others. Me, I'm no good at anything except knowing who is good at what I'm supposed to do.

So what? Just focus on what others are truly superb at, and hire them!

41.

Make Peace with Pugnaciousness

I've yet to meet a sweet, even-tempered individual I didn't want to smack around. How dare they come around with their hearty handshakes and simpering smiles just moments after you've been dumped by the only person on the planet who *really* understands you?

The gall of them.

Do you really want to be like that—be "chipper"? It's an ugly word, isn't it? Why not just settle back and relax into a comfortable state of surliness? Yes, it feels so right.

Keep in mind, nothing is so rewarding as taking out your frustrations on a lesser human being . . . and they're all lesser human beings. Feeling down? Take someone with you. At the end of your tether? Choke a government employee in his own red tape. Need badly to spit nails? Do it for all to see—at the manicurist's or at Home

Depot. As you begin to unleash your anger, you'll discover the true meaning of inner peace.

42.

Work at It—Maybe You Can Fool
a Lot of the People a Lot of the Time

You've probably found nothing in this book difficult to understand. In fact, you've probably said, "Why did I pay $6.95 for this garbage? I could have learned this crap from a Dionne Warwick Psychic Friends infomercial."

Now I'll tell you something you did not know: I had to work very hard to produce this inane little volume.

Writing this book—and all the shallow sequels I'm writing or planning to write—has taught me that the best and most powerful ideas in life can be packaged into megabestsellers if you can strip them entirely of meaning and turn them into shallow nuggets of wisdom. And that's the truth.

43.

Talk Behind People's Backs—Otherwise, When Will You Have a Chance to Talk about Them?

When you've graduated from my course of therapy, you'll not only want to butt into your own business, you'll be butting your nose into everybody else's.

I'm amazed when I hear people advised to "stick to your knitting" or "mind your own beeswax."

The simple, if alarming, truth is that most people are frustrating, bothersome, annoying, and dangerous. They cut you off at the supermarket checkout line, dart in front of you on the highway without signaling, and spank their children in front of shopping-mall cameras.

They would deny it, but most people do

require your intervention! If you don't take action when some-one does something that makes you think, "I can't believe he did that," then you've cheated him, yourself, and society.

Minding your own business is an old wives' tale. Wouldn't you feel delirious if you had jumped in when you saw someone buying the latest Yanni CD? But shame on you, you remained a bystander, not a doer!

It's a wonder people like us don't spend all our time fixing the messes wrought daily by strangers.

44.

Five Reasons Why
Richard Nixon Sweated So Much

1. Knew all along that he should have used eight-track tapes in the White House; if he had, nobody could have played them today.

2. Looked awful in Ban-Lon shirts—and he knew it.

3. Mother said a mustache would make him look shady, even though it would have covered the profusion of perspiration on his upper lip.

4. Did not respond in time to President Kennedy's invitations to party down with the babes of Camelot.

5. Agnew wouldn't let Nixon lower the Oval Office thermostat from eighty-two degrees.

45.

The Greatest American Sweaters
(aside from Dick Nixon, of Course)

1. Patrick Ewing at the foul line twenty seconds after a game begins. He makes the towel-equipped sweat boys under each basket into the NBA's unsung heroes.

2. Monica, Gennifer, and Paula. They might not sweat much, but we know who sweats over them.

3. Men using long-range binoculars to gawk at Pamela Anderson Lee.

4. My brother-in-law Hank. And does he have trouble getting the sweat stains out of his undershirts!

5. Webster Hubbell—President Clinton's good old ex-con Arkansas buddy made his congressional testimony into an

Olympic water sport.

6. Louis Armstrong—No man made nonstop shvitzing classier. He never tried to hide his copious flow; he never ignored it, he never wiped it away with his shirt sleeve as if it were unwelcome. No, he embraced it, deftly mixing his horn play with swift use of the handkerchief, as if the hankie were a member of his band.

46.

Stop Thinking about Your Thoughts

If you were to master one mental exercise of all, it would be to stop the process known as thinking. Dr. Benjamin Whoopee, my mentor, called this "the path of the moron."

One day, he saw my brow furrowed, my eyes fixed and catatonic, and my nostrils flared. "You don't realize the power of your thoughts!" he exclaimed. "You don't even realize you're thinking, but looking at you think made me think, 'Stop that!' The 'path of the moron' tells us to empty our minds, counsel others to do so, and write empty-headed books telling people to stop thinking."

"If I follow you, will I be a moron, too?" I asked.

"Not only that, I'll blurb for your books!"

Years later, Dr. Whoopee fulfilled his promise. For my first book, *Don't Sweat, Turn on the Air-Conditioning*, he wrote: "It made me feel young and stupid all over again!"

47.

Keep Telling Yourself,
"Life Isn't an Emergency"

Hundreds of my clients believe they must get everything done at a breakneck pace.

How many times have I heard them cancel an appointment with this excuse: "I'm sifting through what's left of my possessions in the ashes of the fire that just destroyed my dream house and killed my family. I have to talk to the fire marshal, the insurance adjustor, the undertakers, the burglary squad, and the homicide detectives, and go to my nephew's soccer game."

Usually I say, "And you can't take out fifty minutes to talk about learning how not to think?"

These neurotics! They think they have to clean out their "in-baskets" or their day won't be complete.

Extinguishing fires, staying late at the office, driving the car pool, meeting deadlines, working overtime, passing midterms: they aim so high that they fail to realize that my time is precious.

48.

Just Do It Already!

"Just do it" existed as a phrase long before Nike made it its commercial slogan.

In fact, I invented it.

You see, I can't explain what it is I do. I know that what I do is not very complex, but I can't tell anyone exactly how to be a mumbo-jumbo–spewing writer of sophomoric books full of vapid homilies.

I realize the phrase works well for me. You can read Freud's explanation of his invention of psychotherapy, or Edison's explication of how he fashioned the electric light bulb. Yeesh! What a couple of bores.

People who plan everything are such damned perfectionists! Don't do it. Embrace your flaws and resist the temptation to tell others how you do what you do, especially when you know. Trust that on-off switch inside you that says, "Don't think, just do."

49.

Pretend the Other Person's Inane
Argument Makes Sense

I've always felt that a good disagreement fosters the flow of good ideas and sometimes the flow of blunt objects.

But lately, I've noticed how rude I've become, robotically objecting to heinous, inane, antisocial ideas. But I've learned to change. Suppose your wife tells you, "I think Willie Nelson is the cutest guy I've ever seen."

Instead of responding with the obvious, knee-jerk response of any normal male, think of saying, "Gosh, honey, any average, hard-working guy can see what's adorable about an unshaven, ponytailed, marijuana-smokin', scruffy sexagenarian who spends most of his time on a bus."

The tone of your statement makes all the difference in how she will respond. Don't correct your wife or offer every shred of proof to show she's wrong. Pretend to be a good listener. Nod your head knowingly. Take notes.

I have found it extremely energizing to listen to a miscreant say incredibly stupid things. But by responding adequately you will have momentarily halted the spiral of stupidity.

50.

Imagine Yourself at the Funeral of Someone You Hated

I was amazed when, after my father died, my stepmother buried him naked in a very long, unadorned orange crate.

"Why?" I asked. "I've never been to a funeral," the prune-faced, droopy septugenarian lied. Well, most of us will attend many funerals, for people we like, for people we may not know very well, and sometimes for those we hate.

Most likely, the loathed corpse will be the aunt who stiffed you on a gift at your bat mitzvah, or the grandfather whose idea of fun was to pinch the supple tushies of neighborhood girls. So how do you get through a funeral without sweat?

- Bring enough balloons for the people in your row to make into a life-size replica of the deceased.

- Put naked pictures of the deceased on the World Wide Web.

- In the hours before the service, sneak into the funeral home and make up the deceased to look like Fester Addams.

- Change the processional music from a Brahms concerto to something more respectful by Snoop Doggy Dogg.

51.

Understand the Statement, "You're Damned if You Do and You Do if You Do"

This is the title of a superb self-help book by Dr. Norm Crosby. It means there's no way out, no matter what you do, even if you do it and can do it better than anyone else. If you work hard to raise a child or win a promotion, you are doomed to failure, no matter what.

We believe that when we try hard, with the purest of intentions, we will be rewarded with cash, as if we came closest to Bob Barker's price without exceeding it.

But Dr. Crosby counsels us that we can never climb out of our purgatories even with a good ladder from Home Depot. We may get tantalizing peeks at the promised land. Those peeks are called hope. Hope is merely a tease, an illusion designed to make us work harder, run farther, and jump higher.

A marvelous thing happens when we realize that even if we

do what we do—and do it better than anyone else has ever dreamed of doing it—we're damned, no matter what we do.

52.

Think Nice Thoughts
about Really Awful People

H ow many times have you heard it said of a serial murderer, "Poor old Jeffrey Dahmer—he didn't know what he was doing"? If so, you've been exposed to the sagacity of "looking beyond bad behavior."

You do it for your kids, even if they burn down your house. Why not for the worst among us?

Wouldn't it be nice if we could try to believe what neighbors say of mass murderers: "A nice man," "a quiet man," and "a fine newspaper delivery boy despite the human limbs that fell out of the Sunday paper."

"Looking beyond bad behavior" doesn't mean whistling a happy tune when Mel the Pharmacist shoots up his pals at the soda fountain. It simply means remembering that after sweating for so long in a simmering silence, Mel had ruined all his T-shirts and had no recourse but to take swift action.

Sticking your head in the sand is easier than you think.

53.

Remember, "The Journey of a Thousand Miles Begins with a Single Step" (I Made that Quote Up, You Know)

E ven today, I can remember the first sentence I wrote in my first book. "Call me Ishmael." It still rings true! And then I wrote: "I shall return." It seems so long ago! Yet, had I not written that first sentence, I wouldn't have found the next, now cited by Bartlett's. "And so it goes," I wrote next.

Sometimes, when you consider appropriating other people's possessions—their words, their shoes, or their pants—the task can seem daunting. You feel like you'll be caught and sentenced to pick up roadside trash with men named Big Louise.

The trick to overcoming your reservations is to take something small to start. Like a verb. After a few verbs, pilfer some nouns. Pretty soon, you've got your own sentence!

Over and over, I hear of projects people say they will start, but never do. It is then I think of something I said: "In the Beginning was the Word, and then a phrase, then a sentence, a paragraph, and an essay answer to the midterm question." And I was good.

54.

Resist the Urge Not to Criticize

The Rev. Mike Ditka of the New Orleans Diocese reminds us that criticism is a transformative experience, that when we tear into somebody in full view of thousands of people, we make a very big point.

I remember watching Mike during his weekly televised confessional. A sinner confessed, "Forgive me, Father, I have done connubial things with my sister-in-law, I cheated on my civil service test, and I haven't paid taxes since 1983."

Before his cable TV audience, Rev. Mike tore down the confessional screen and screamed, "You freaking moron, don't you know right from wrong? Has your brain forgotten you? Didn't you study the playbook?" Rev. Mike then ordered the unconditional release of the man from our successful congregation.

If you let people around you work ignorantly, you lose. Stupidity and sloppiness are habits that can be overcome only when you make criticism an integral part of your life.

55.
Count to Ten

When I was young, my father used to count out loud to ten when he was angry with my sisters and me. Sometimes, he made it straight through to ten, but he usually skipped eight.

I've worked hard to improve my father's counting strategy to include eight, and to add the concept of breathing between numbers. (I wonder if I can patent it?)

When you feel angry, take a long, deep breath, and say the number one. Exhale. When you've mastered that, take a long, deep breath, then exhale into the nearest balloon.

Repeat this until the count of ten, twenty, or even thirty. You'll have several nice balloon animals—even balloon people if you've got talented breath—and that should ease your troubles. If you're still angry, puncture 'em all with a pin, an exercise that will show you how, in the blink of an eye, the "big stuff" can turn into "small, torn, broken stuff."

56.

If You Love Your Plant,
You May Learn to Love Your Hideous Boss

For some people, loving a plant is a lot easier than loving a pet or a person. A plant doesn't ask for money, an education, designer jeans, or the latest Playstation video game.

It only wants water.

But that fat, loud, verbally abusive boor who is your supervisor is much harder to love. (So is your fat, loud, verbally abusive, badly-dressed spouse, for that matter.)

The goal is to practice your love on your plant. It could be thriving or drooping. Start by talking to it. Tell it your hopes and dreams. Take it on rides to the country. Caress it. Buy it an occasional gift, maybe a brooch. Promise to marry it in a big church wedding.

Notice how you feel. You are in your loving place. You've given this plant unconditional love. You're never unhappy when you're loving the plant. You're at peace.

Shortly, you'll be able to expand your network of love beyond your plant. Even·when your boorish boss is forcing you to participate in a project beneath you, think of the plant.

Love your boss as you would love it. Just don't forget to water the cretin, with special attention to his toupee.

57.
Dr. Feelgood's Guide to Feeling Good No. 4

1. Test-drive a Bentley, taking corners at ninety-five miles per hour.

2. Enroll in a baseball-fantasy camp, mug Tommy Lasorda.

3. Wear a Styrofoam cheese head to your first day at the office.

4. Stop, smell, and steal someone else's roses.

5. Tell your patients to make more money.

58.
Food for Thought

The other day, I was waiting in line at the local bakery to get the last available chocolate cream pie. I waited patiently, but just as I was ready to order the pie, the jerk in front of me piped up and ordered it first.

As you might imagine, I was outraged. But he merely shrugged off my verbal protests with a simple, "Hey, pal—tough luck. That's the way the cookie crumbles."

Still angered by this sudden turn of events, I began to ponder a crumbling cookie and just what that expression really meant. I thought about it more and more, and ultimately came to the conclusion that it didn't mean anything. That realization just set me off again.

So I ran off to find that jerk with the last pie. I found him in the parking lot, grabbed the pie out of his car, and smacked him in the face with it. He, of course, was absolutely stunned and surprised. But as I walked off, feeling good about what

I'd done, I tried to think of some other time-worn expression, saying, or cliché to underscore my actions.

But I was so angry I couldn't think of anything clever. So I simply yelled, "Hey mister . . . up yours with your crumbly cookie!"

59.
Give Up the Fear of Repeating Yourself

People were so enamored of my first book that I see no reason not to keep giving them what they want. And that's a lesson for all of you: Why toil endlessly thinking of brand-new ideas, techniques, or methods to achieve a goal only to forget what got you where you are? Believe me, I'll never forget; I've been working about an hour a day to come up with these ideas for my next books, which will be in bookstores shortly:

- *Don't Sweat the Small Stuff . . . for Your In-Law Children*

- *Don't Sweat the Small Stuff . . . For Children Born Out of Wedlock*

- *Don't Sweat the Small Stuff . . . For Our Hasidic Friends in Long Black Coats*

- *Ageless Body, Sweatless Pore*

- *Start Sweating the Delta Burke–Size Stuff*
- *The Seven Deodorants of Highly Odious People*
- *Think and Grow Fat*

About the Authors

Richard Sandomir recently had his small stuff surgically removed. He remains able to perform the work required to be the TV sports columnist for the *New York Times*.

Rick Wolff orders his favorite deodorant in bulk every month, which benefits every person he works with as a senior editor for Warner Books.

Sandomir and Wolff are veteran parody writers, and collaborated on the humor classic, *Life for Real Dummies*. On his own, Wolff wrote *Sports Illstated* and *Golf Dirty Tricks*. Sandomir is the author of *Bald Like Me*.